This
David Bennett Book
belongs to

Jessica   Daley

First published in paperback in 1993
by David Bennett Books Ltd,
94 Victoria Street, St Albans,
Herts, AL1 3TG.
First published in hardback in 1991
by Kingfisher Books

Consultant: Dr Julian Hector

BRITISH LIBRARY CATALOGUING IN PUBLICATION DATA
A catalogue record for this book is available
from the British Library.
ISBN 1 85602 053 3

Typesetting by Type City
Production by Imago
Printed in Hong Kong

I am a Rabbit

Written by
Linda Bygrave

Illustrated by
Louise Voce

David Bennett Books

I am a rabbit.
I am small with two long ears,
thick fur and strong back legs.

I also have a short, white fluffy tail.

I like to hop about.
The thick hair on the soles
of my feet gives me a good grip.

My thick coat of fur protects
my body. It grows even thicker
in winter to keep me nice and warm.

I like to live with lots of friends.
We eat and play in grassy places.

I make my home under the ground.
It is called a burrow.

This is my burrow with places to run
and places to pass each other.

There are also rooms for sleeping
and a nursery for the babies.

I stay in the burrow most of the day.
I come out at night to feed and play.

I use my teeth and claws to keep
myself very clean.

Most of the time, I eat grass.
But I also eat the farmer's vegetables
if I can find some.

In winter, when there is no grass
or vegetables, I eat the bark
from trees.

I am a mummy rabbit.
Over there is a daddy rabbit.
We look quite alike, don't we?

We're feeling excited because
we are going to have some babies.
Lots and lots of babies!

I have my babies when it is warm.
Usually, I have between three and
eight of them at once.

Each lot of babies is called a litter.
At first, they can't see or hear.

After about ten days my babies can see.
Now they have more fur
and they can move and hear well.

Once they are about two weeks old,
we leave the burrow for the first time.
We meet lots of other rabbits.

We must be careful! We have
enemies. If we keep very still,
it is hard for them to see us.

I can move my ears backwards or forwards
without moving the rest of my body.
This way I can hear if an enemy is coming.

My eyes are on the sides of my head.
I can keep a lookout all around me
without moving my head.

If an enemy does come near, the oldest daddy rabbit thumps the ground hard with his feet. Then we all run home.

When they are one month old,
my babies can look after themselves.
They don't need me anymore.

I carry on feeding and playing,
and having more babies.
That is why there are so many rabbits.
Goodbye!

Other David Bennett paperbacks you will enjoy . . .

I am a Duck *Linda Bygrave • Louise Voce*　　　　　　*ISBN 1 85602 054 1*

I am a Frog *Linda Bygrave • Louise Voce*　　　　　　*ISBN 1 85602 051 7*

I am a Butterfly *Linda Bygrave • Louise Voce*　　　　*ISBN 1 85602 052 5*

I am a Rabbit *Linda Bygrave • Louise Voce*　　　　　*ISBN 1 85602 053 3*

As featured on BBC TV's *Playdays*. The perfect nature library for the very young.

If Dinosaurs Came To Town *Dom Mansell*　　　　　*ISBN 1 85602 044 4*

'. . . combines detailed pictures and evocative language with inviting tit-bits of science' *The Independent*

The Monster Book of ABC Sounds *Alan Snow*　　　*ISBN 1 85602 041 X*

An ABC of sounds, which follows a riotous game of hide-and-seek between a group of rats and monsters.

Inside Big Machines *Arlene Blanchard • Tony Wells*　　*ISBN 1 85602 043 6.*

A fascinating look inside some of the world's biggest machines.

Teddy Bear, Teddy Bear *Carol Lawson*　　　　　　*ISBN 1 85602 040 1*

A beautifully illustrated version of the classic children's activity rhyme.

One Cow Moo Moo! *David Bennett • Andy Cooke*　　*ISBN 1 85602 042 8*

As featured on BBC TV's *Over The Moon*. A farmyard romp through numbers from one to ten.